The My

Missing Big Wig

Written by Jill Eggleton
Illustrated by Trevor Pye

Mickey Maloney, the spy,
was looking for his boss, Big Wig.
He phoned, he faxed,
he e-mailed, he text-messaged!

But . . .

Big Wig had vanished,
like fleas on a dog.

Mickey Maloney
scratched his head
and rubbed his eye.
"This job is for
a **SUPERIOR SPY!**
That's me!" he said.

So Mickey Maloney went spying!
He got on a bus, and
took out his spyglass.

"I'm looking for Big Wig,
the captain, the chief.
Big Wig, the boss of the spies.
Big Wig has vanished,
like fleas on a dog.
Is he somewhere here
in disguise?"

The people on the bus shouted,

"Shivering shudders!
Big Wig is on this bus?"

So. . .

they patted and prodded and jabbed and jiggled, pulled and poked and wrenched and wiggled.
But no one on the bus was Big Wig.

Big Wig had vanished, like ice in the sun.

Mickey Maloney
got off the bus, and
all the people did, too.

He went into a shop and
took out his spyglass.

"I'm looking for Big Wig,
the captain, the chief.
Big Wig, the boss of the spies.
Big Wig has vanished,
like ice in the sun.
Is he somewhere here
in disguise?"

The people in the shop said,

"Shivering shudders!
Big Wig is in this shop?"

So. . .

they patted and prodded and jabbed and jiggled, pulled and poked and wrenched and wiggled. But no one in the shop was Big Wig.

Big Wig had vanished, like smoke in the wind.

Mickey Maloney
went out of the shop, and
all the people did, too.

He went into the library and
took out his spyglass.

"I'm looking for Big Wig,
the captain, the chief.
Big Wig, the boss of the spies.
Big Wig has vanished,
like smoke in the wind.
Is he somewhere here
in disguise?"

Shhh!

The people in the library shouted,

"Shivering shudders!
Big Wig is in this library?"

So. . .

they patted and prodded and jabbed and jiggled, pulled and poked and wrenched and wiggled.
But no one in the library was Big Wig.

Big Wig had vanished, like ants in a crack.

Spies
by
I.C.U.

Mickey Maloney
scratched his head and
rubbed his eye.
"This is a job for
HUNDREDS of spies!"
he said.

And all the people shouted,
"We'll help!

We'll sneak and snoop
and peer and pry!
We'll hunt and track
and ferret and spy!

We'll find Big Wig!"

So off went Mickey Maloney
and all the people.

They looked for Big Wig
up mountains.
They looked for Big Wig
in deserts.
They looked for Big Wig
in jungles.
No Big Wig!

The people said,
“Big Wig has vanished,
like dust in the sand!”

“**Sand!**” said Mickey Maloney.
“I know where Big Wig is!”

So Mickey Maloney and
all the people went to
the Island of Loafers.

They saw Big Wig lying
on the sand.
He was singing . . .

"I'm Big Wig the chief,
the boss of the spies.
But no one will know me
in this disguise!"

So Mickey Maloney leapt out from the trees and shouted, **"SURPRISE! SURPRISE!"**

"Shivering shudders!"

said Big Wig.
"I thought I had vanished, like a snake down a hole."

"Not from me!"
said Mickey Maloney.
"I'm a **SUPERIOR** spy!"

Guide Notes

Title: The Mystery of Missing Big Wig
Stage: Year 4

Genre: Fiction
Approach: Shared Reading
Processes: Thinking Critically, Exploring Language, Processing Information
Written and Visual Focus: Change of Text Style and Font, Illustrative Text

THINKING CRITICALLY

(sample questions)

- Why do you think a superior spy was needed to find Big Wig?
- Why do you think the people said, "Shivering shudders!" when they thought Big Wig was there?
- Why do you think Big Wig wanted to vanish?
- What else do you think Mickey Maloney could have done to find Big Wig in a hurry?
- What do you think made Mickey Maloney go to the Island of Loafers?
- Why do you think the Island was called the "Island of Loafers"?
- Why do you think Mickey Maloney was so anxious to find Big Wig?
- What parts of this story make it fictional?

EXPLORING LANGUAGE

Terminology

Title, cover, illustrations, author, illustrator

Vocabulary

Interest words: superior, prodded, jabbed, jiggled, wrenched, wiggled, disguise, sneak, snoop, peer, pry, ferret
Silent letter: wrenched
Singular/Plural: spy/spies, person/people
Antonyms: superior/inferior
Homonyms: peer/peer, ferret/ferret
Homophone: piece/peace
Synonyms: vanished/disappeared, wrenched/tugged, boss/chief, sneak/snoop
Simile: vanished – like ice in the sun/like smoke in the wind
Alliteration: shivering shudders

Print Conventions

Exclamation marks, quotation marks, commas, question marks, ellipses, apostrophes